MW00809967

IMAGES
of America

GHOST TOWNS
AND MINING CAMPS
OF SOUTHERN NEVADA

During the early development of Rhyolite and Bullfrog, freight wagons were essential. Here a load of freight heads out from Bullfrog in December 1905. To the right is the first two-story building constructed in the area. A year later, the first railroad arrived at Rhyolite. By 1907, Rhyolite and Bullfrog had a population of more than 6,000. (CNHS.)

ON THE COVER: After the discoveries at Rhyolite during the summer of 1904, people began flocking to the area. The valley quickly became dotted with hundreds of wood-framed tents. Once it was determined that the ore was going to last, the tents were replaced by first wood, then stone, buildings. (CNHS.)

IMAGES
of America

GHOST TOWNS
AND MINING CAMPS
OF SOUTHERN NEVADA

Shawn Hall

ARCADIA
PUBLISHING

Published by Arcadia Publishing
Charleston, South Carolina

Library of Congress Control Number: 209922884

For all general information contact Arcadia Publishing at:
Telephone 843-853-2070
Fax 843-853-0044
E-mail sales@arcadiapublishing.com
For customer service and orders:
Toll-Free 1-888-313-2665

Visit us on the Internet at www.arcadiapublishing.com

*This book is lovingly dedicated to my beautiful daughter,
Heather Ashley Hall. You truly are the sunshine of my life!*

CONTENTS

ACKNOWLEDGMENTS

First, I would like to thank my family for supporting my writing endeavors and often participating in my ghost town adventures. Writing this book came at a difficult time since I lost my father, Al Hall, in October 2008. My mother, Lorraine, and my daughter, Heather, have provided comfort and support during this difficult time. Thank you so much.

I also want to thank Eva LaRue of the Central Nevada Museum, who helped immensely in pulling together historical photographs for this book. We have been good friends for many years, and I greatly appreciate that. Without her help, I would not have been able to gather all the photographs that I needed.

Many other friends in the history and museum fields have been instrumental in my success in writing about the history of the great state of Nevada: Bob Nylen (curator of history at the Nevada State Museum), Doug and Cindy Southerland of Southerland Studios (SS), Howard Hickson (retired director of the Northeastern Nevada Museum), the Metscher brothers (Bill, Philip, and Allen—founders of the Central Nevada Museum), Wally Cuchine (Eureka Opera House), Gloria Harjes, and many others. I would also like to add a special thank-you to Debbie Seracini, of Arcadia Publishing, for serving as the editor of my text.

I also need to thank my all of my many ghost-towning friends who have shared adventures with me. Cat House, Bruce Franchini, Charlie Hall, Stanley Paher, Dave Toby, and many others have made exploring Nevada's historic ghost towns a wonderful experience. I would also like to thank my "true" friends in Tonopah, who supported me during and particularly after my time as director of the Tonopah Historic Mining Park.

There are strict word limitations for books in this Arcadia series, so to allow myself to provide more historical information, credit for photographs from the Central Nevada Museum and Central Historical Society are shown as CNHS. Most of the other photographs used were either taken by myself or are part of my historical photograph collection. These are credited simply as SRH. Any other photographs will have a full credit shown.

INTRODUCTION

Visiting ghost towns and mining towns continues to be a growing hobby for many people. Nevada provides fertile ground for this activity with its mainly rural and remote nature; many ghost towns still have a lot of remnants to explore. But what exactly is a ghost town? The best definition I have found is by Lambert Florin, a legendary ghost town enthusiast, who said a ghost town is a "shadowy semblance of a former self." There are a number of towns in Nevada that have had previous populations in the thousands and might only have a handful of residents left. Some of these towns still serve as county seats. However, since those are also mining towns, they can be classified as either.

There are more than 1,500 ghost towns in Nevada. Some are places that only existed for a few months, and others only died after 50 or more years. They are scattered throughout every corner, mountain, and valley in the state. That means one can plan a trip of any length to visit many special places. Just a friendly warning: once people start exploring these fascinating historic sites, there is a very strong danger that they will catch what ghost town enthusiasts call "ghost town fever." I caught it back in 1979 and am still happily afflicted with it.

Unfortunately, while most visitors are responsible when exploring, there has been a disturbing trend of theft and destruction by some. This is reprehensible and should not be tolerated by any true ghost town enthusiast. If anyone should witness such activities, please take the time to report it to the authorities. These places are the windows into our past and need to be preserved for future generations to enjoy. My simple rule is "take only photographs." With the rise in value of antique mining equipment, vandals, who have no interest in history, are stripping these valuable icons of the American West that, once gone, can never be replaced.

Southern Nevada has a rich mining history and provides a wonderful place to explore. Many of these old mining towns are located on main highways, which gives those who do not have access to a four-wheel-drive vehicle the opportunity to step into the past. Mining began in earnest in southern Nevada during the early 1860s as a result of the huge ore strikes in Virginia City. Once all of the mining ground there was taken, prospectors began fanning out eastward to the unexplored interior of Nevada. Places like Belmont, Aurora, Manhattan, Candelaria, Silver Peak, and Tybo came into existence during the 1860s and 1870s. Production from these early southern towns had a lot to do with the development of the new state of Nevada.

Unfortunately, during the late 1880s and throughout the 1890s, there was a deep depression of the mining industries. Most shut down and activity was limited. This culminated with the financial panic of 1893 and a collapse in the price of silver. With the huge gold strikes in the Yukon and Alaska in 1897, most of the unemployed miners headed north to make their living. The state of Nevada teetered on the brink of bankruptcy. However, the huge strikes made early in the new century at Tonopah and Goldfield breathed life back into the struggling economy. With the incredible amounts of silver and gold being produced, the state of Nevada was finally able to shake off the doldrums of the past 20 years. These two towns brought back prosperity to many different industries throughout the state. New railroads and mills were built, demand for agriculture products rose dramatically, and new businesses opened to satisfy demand. The advent of motorized vehicles also had a dramatic impact on development. Other mining towns developed like Manhattan, Rhyolite and Johnnie boomed, and older towns like Candelaria, Tybo, and Silver Peak enjoyed a resurgence.

The financial panic of 1907 put a damper on the boom. This was caused by the San Francisco earthquake of 1906 and also the federal government establishing maximum rates for the railroads. Most of Tonopah's financial backing came from San Francisco businessmen. Many historians agree that it was the rich flow of silver from Tonopah that helped rebuild the destroyed city. As a result of the panic, most of the mining towns in southern Nevada shut down. However, the mainstay mines in Tonopah and Goldfield continued to operate at a high level and helped save the state once again. These two towns were the only places in southern Nevada that still enjoyed substantial production during the ensuing years.

Soon even those two towns began to slow down. Goldfield peaked in 1910 with production of $10.7 million, and by 1920, all major operations had ceased. Tonopah fared a little better, continuing to produce ore until World War II, although by the end of the 1920s, production was a mere shadow of what it had been during its heyday. Virtually all mining was curtailed during World War II as a result of government regulations allowing only essential war minerals to be mined. After the war, with prices extremely low, very little mining activity restarted. All the remaining railroads serving southern Nevada folded, further isolating the mining towns.

Throughout Nevada's mining history, there has been a strong pattern of bonanza and borrasca, periods of incredible production followed by an extended period of depression. For southern Nevada, the post–World War II period was long on borrasca and short on bonanza. As the population of the United States became more mobile and began traveling more and more, many of these old mining towns began to rely on tourism and travelers to stay alive, utilizing their remoteness to become centers for people to get gas, eat, and pick up supplies. Southern Nevada did have an advantage over other struggling areas in Nevada: the U.S. military. With the establishment of the Nevada Test Site, many residents of rural towns were able to find work there and still do today.

During the past 20 years, there have been a number of large open-pit mining operations that have come and gone, bringing temporary booms to the local economy. Tonopah enjoyed the benefit of being the home for the Stealth fighter program during the 1980s and early 1990s. However, when that program was moved to New Mexico, the town's population went from over 5,000 to less than 3,000. For all of the existing towns in southern Nevada, it is still a roller-coaster ride of survival. However, residents keep hope alive, hoping for the next bonanza to start at any time.

One

TONOPAH

Jim Butler, a local rancher, discovered silver ore here on May 19, 1900. He and his wife, Belle, filed eight claims. Six of these—Desert Queen, Burro, Valley View, Silver Top, Buckboard, and Mizpah—turned into some of the biggest producers the state has ever had. Tonopah began to grow by leaps and bounds.

By January 1901, there were 40 men in the camp. Within weeks, the population had grown to 250. The mines around the town produced almost $750,000 in gold and silver in 1901, and for the next 40 years, the Tonopah mines were consistent producers. Population peaked around 7,000.

The Tonopah Railroad, completed in 1904, connected Tonopah to the Carson and Colorado Railroad at Sodaville. The rails were extended to Goldfield in the fall of 1905, and the railroad was renamed the Tonopah and Goldfield Railroad. In May 1905, Tonopah became the county seat.

Tonopah's mines maintained a high yearly production until the Depression brought a slowdown. Mine production from 1900 to 1921 was almost $121 million. All production ceased at the beginning of World War II, and in 1947, the Tonopah and Goldfield Railroad folded. Tonopah now has a population of about 2,800.

During recent times, the town's proximity to the Nellis Air Force Bombing and Gunnery Range supported the town. Tonopah was home to the super-secret Stealth fighters and bombers. When the Stealth base was relocated to New Mexico in the 1990s, Tonopah lost almost half of its population.

Tourism now plays a large part in the local economy. Many historic buildings remain in the town. Two museums are in Tonopah: the Tonopah Historic Mining Park and the Central Nevada Museum. Both have many displays and thousands of mining artifacts. The mining park features a walking tour through its 110-acre property, which features original head frames, mining buildings, and an underground tour. The Central Nevada Museum has an outdoor ghost town comprised of old buildings saved from destruction from the local area. Both provide a wonderful look at Tonopah's vibrant mining past.

FORMERLY A DESERT
NOW TONOPAH

A. L. Smith, Tonopah, photo
$2,000,000 WORTH OF ORE AT ONE VIEW

HAVE you ever seen $2,000,000 in values piled up out of doors and readily accessible? You have seen great buildings, battleships, bridges, and other finished products of human energy and skill worth more money perhaps; but here you see a part of this great wealth in the crude, the ore dump of the Tonopah Company from the Brougher Shaft, containing 35,000 tons of ore worth from $30 to $100 per ton. Look closely and you will see other smaller ore dumps, the property of those pioneers of Tonopah, the leasers, some of whom landed in Tonopah from freight teams with less than the price of a week's board, now nearly all men of wealth; and what you see there is some of that wealth not yet turned into money.

We invite you to come to Tonopah. We will take you to a place where you can see more than $2,000,000 worth of ore at one view, and this is less than one-twentieth of that ready and waiting under the surface to be brought to light before long by an army of men assisted by great engines and tons of dynamite.

We will show you also the gray ore dumps of the Belmont to the east, the white ore dumps of the North Star to the northeast, the blue ore dumps of the Montana Tonopah to the north, the brown ore dumps of the Midway to the west, and still farther west, down on the edge of the desert, the mines that have but recently caught the great veins, the Tonopah Extension and the MacNamara. West of these no man can tell what wealth may be uncovered by the Red Rock, the Pittsburg, the Great Western, and others of that little array of mines steadily working toward the setting sun.

You will not believe what we can tell you of Tonopah and its nearly as wonderful neighbors without seeing for yourself.

COME TO TONOPAH AND LET US SHOW YOU.

Tonopah Railroad Company opened July 25, 1904.

CITIZENS OF TONOPAH, NYE COUNTY, NEVADA

As soon as Tonopah was established, a large promotional campaign was launched. Because of the remoteness of the town, it was a challenge to attract miners to work in the mines. With so much rich ore available, mine owners needed to get it out quick. As a result, miners were offered some of the highest wages available in the West. (SRH.)

The founder of Tonopah, Jim Butler, poses with his mule. Legend has it that when Butler was camping at Tonopah Springs, he got angry at the mule, picked up a rock to throw at him, and realized that the weight of the rock was odd. It was solid silver, and the rest is history. (SRH.)

By early 1901, the town of Tonopah was still in its infancy. Most of the structures in town were still wood-framed tents, but the transition had started, as a few wood structures were being built on what would become Main Street. Population at this time was only around 200, but it had ballooned to 1,000 by the end of the year. (CNHS.)

A freight wagon unloads at Tonopah during the spring of 1901. Lack of nearby wood slowed initial construction until freight lines became established, and many businesses were housed in tents. On the slopes of the mountain in the background, the development of the town's major mines is just getting underway. (CNHS.)

BARREL HOUSE, TONOPAH, NEV.

Because of the low supply and high expense of lumber, residents of Tonopah scrounged for anything that would make a home to protect against the cold winter wind. Here the choice was old water barrels. When filled with dirt, they would provide some insulation. High on the mountain, the North Star Mine is visible. (SRH.)

While this might look like a nice cut-stone house, it is actually made from empty 5-gallon oil cans. The oil was used for lubrication in the milling equipment, and there was always a constant supply of the cans. Inventive miners wanting to construct a cheap home took advantage. (SRH.)

With the large amount of saloons during Tonopah's early years, empty beer bottles were also in supply. This home was built with 10,000 bottles, carefully chinked with adobe. Unfortunately, a number of years ago, the building was torn down to sell the bottles. A number of other bottle houses were built in other mining towns in southern Nevada. (SRH.)

By 1902, Tonopah was starting to look like a permanent town. The main street was lined with businesses, and a few multistory buildings had been constructed. Mining was really hitting its stride. On the hillside in the background, the new steel head frame of the mighty Mizpah Mine overlooks the boomtown. (CNHS.)

The entire population of Tonopah gathered on Main Street in 1902 for this photograph. This view gives a good feel about how far the town's development had progressed in only two years. The street is lined with wood-framed buildings, and all of the tent businesses are now gone. The future was bright indeed for the town. (SS.)

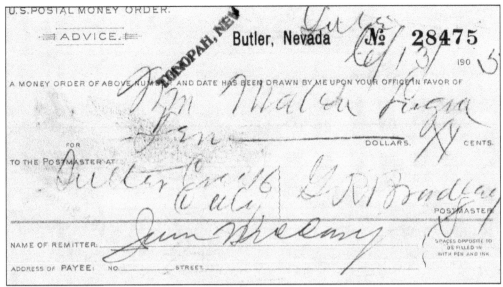

This money order shows a stamp of "Tonopah, Nev" over the original town name of Butler. The name was change to Tonopah after the postmaster general determined that there were already too many towns called Butler with post offices and told the townspeople they would have to choose another name. (SRH.)

The Northern Saloon, located on Main Street, was owned by Wyatt Earp. Legend has it that one time he went to a friend's claim to find him being harassed by a couple of thugs. Earp told them to leave, and they said, "Who do you think you are?" He told them; they turned white and ran away, never to be seen in Tonopah again. (CNHS.)

The Brougher building was the first three-story building constructed in Tonopah. It housed the Tonopah Bank and a hotel. The Mizpah Grill next door would later be razed to make way for the construction of one of the most modern hotels of its era, the Mizpah Hotel. The Brougher building still stands today. (SS.)

Tonopah became well known for its Fourth of July celebrations. This one from 1903 shows miners participating in a drilling contest. These events were extremely popular, and the tradition continues today. The Nevada State Mining Championships still take place in Tonopah during Jim Butler Days, held over Memorial Day weekend. (SRH.)

Silver was being produced by the ton from the mines. This tabletop of silver bricks, worth $250,000 at the time, is ready for shipment on the railroad's Wells Fargo car, which was guarded by a team of agents. The silver was cast in 100-pound bricks to prevent any of them from "walking off." (SS.)

The Mizpah Mine was the mainstay of the Tonopah Mining Company, which produced more than $47 million during its lifetime. This figure is based on the silver price at the time, which was 40¢ an ounce. Now it is worth more than $1.7 billion. To the right is the head frame, in the middle is the hoist house, and at left is the four-story ore bin, the largest in Tonopah. (SRH.)

The Tonopah Extension Mine was another major producer at Tonopah. It was active from 1904 to 1939 and produced $22 million at 40¢ an ounce. Charles Schwab, of investment fame, was the owner of the company for many years. The company had a 60-stamp mill to process its ore. (SRH.)

The Montana Tonopah Mine was another prominent Tonopah mine. While it was only active from 1903 until 1925, it did produce $9.3 million in ore. The huge mill, steel head frame, and other surface buildings were dismantled shortly after the closure. The site is now part of the Tonopah Historic Mining Park. (SRH.)

The five-story Mizpah Hotel has always been the centerpiece structure of Tonopah. The hotel was completed in 1908 and cost $200,000 to construct. It boasted baths, steam heat, and elevators. In the 1980s, the hotel underwent a $1-million restoration. However, the Mizpah has been closed for a number of years and awaits a new owner. (SRH.)

The arrival of the railroad in Tonopah on July 25, 1904, was met with great fanfare and a three-day celebration. Having a railroad greatly accelerated the town's growth because more ore was able to be shipped compared to the slow pace it took horse-drawn wagons. Goods also were able to flow freely into town to aid in its expansion. (SRH.)

Public Library, Tonopah, Nev.

Citizens were very proud when the town library opened in 1912. The library is still used today and is the oldest continuously operating community library in Nevada. It was built using locally quarried stone and was recently restored. A new addition has been built to better serve its patrons. (SRH.)

U. S. S. TONOPAH

Monitor. Built by Bath Iron Works, Bath, Maine. Submarine Tender, Atlantic Fleet. Length over all, 255 ft. 1 in; Beam, 50 ft.; Tonnage, 3225 tons; Guns, 2·12 in., 4·4 in., 2·6 lbs. Crew, 31 officers, 195 men. Speed, 13.04 knots. [OVER]

In 1900, the monitor USS *Nevada* was launched. However, in 1909, it was renamed the USS *Tonopah* so a new battle ship could be commissioned as the USS *Nevada*. Residents took pride in their ship and followed its adventures. Tonopah was one of very few towns that had the honor of a ship named for it. The ship was decommissioned in 1920 and was later sold for scrap. (SRH.)

As Tonopah continued to boom, it was necessary to build a much larger school. A very attractive two-story wood building was constructed. It served for many years until a new high school was built in the 1950s. The building remained empty for years and was finally torn down because of safety issues. (SS.)

After the railroad arrived in Tonopah, spurs were run to many of the major mines, which allowed for easy transport of ore. Here flatbed cars are loaded with sacks of ore from the Tonopah Extension Mine to be taken for processing at mills located 10 miles west of town. (SRH.)

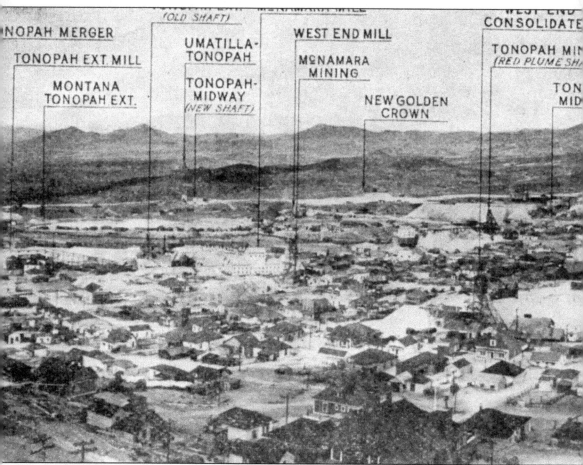

NOPAH MERGER

TONOPAH EXT. MILL

MONTANA
TONOPAH EXT.

(OLD SHAFT)

UMATILLA-
TONOPAH

TONOPAH-
MIDWAY
(NEW SHAFT)

WEST END MILL

McNAMARA
MINING

NEW GOLDEN
CROWN

WEST END
CONSOLIDATE

TONOPAH MIN
(RED PLUME SH

TON
MID

Tonopah was at its peak in the early 1910s, when this photograph was taken. By this time, Tonopah was a true city in all aspects. Taken looking north, the image shows all the major mines and mills. Note how some of the mines are located in the middle of town. The Mizpah Hotel and the adjacent Belvada building dominate the downtown section. The Tonopah Belmont Mine and Mill are located over the crest of the hill. This was the scene of the deadliest mine accident

GYPSY QUEEN

MONTANA-
TONOPAH
(MILL)

TONOPAH MINING
(MIZPAH SHAFT)

MONTANA TONOPAH MINE

NORTH STAR

TONOPAH BELMONT
(OLD SHAFT)

TONOPAH BELMO
(MINE AND MILL)

TONOPAH MININ
(DESERT QUEEN SHA

in Tonopah's history. Tragedy struck on February 28, 1911. A mysterious fire, small but smoky, broke out at the bottom of the 1,200-foot shaft of the Belmont Mine at 7:00 in the morning. Although many men were brought to safety, 17 men perished in the mine, including "Big" Bill Murphy, who saved numerous men by riding down the shaft and pulling them to safety before perishing on his last trip. (SRH.)

The Tonopah and Goldfield Railroad depot in lower Tonopah was a busy place in 1912. The depot stood empty after the railroad folded in the late 1940s. In 1979, the Central Nevada Museum had worked everything out to restore the building for use as the museum. However, arson claimed the building in October 1980 before work started. (SRH.)

Here is a view of the Mizpah Mine in the 1940s after mining had ended. During the 1950s and 1960s, Howard Hughes had control of most of Tonopah's old mines. He spent much of his time living here, experimenting with improvements to the Hughes drill and attempting to find ways to increase ore recovery rates. During his time here, Hughes married his second wife, Jean Peters, in a local motel. (SRH.)

This is a modern-day view of the Desert Queen Mine. This is one of only two wooden head frames remaining in Tonopah. It also has a complete hoist house with all of the original engines and equipment inside. Unfortunately, the head frame is in danger as its support legs are rotting through, and unless it undergoes restoration very soon, this rare and beautiful artifact of Tonopah's past will be lost. (Lorraine Hall.)

The Mizpah head frame, one of the first steel frames built in Nevada, has undergone two different restorations during the past five years and is ready to continue overlooking the town of Tonopah for many years to come. The hoist house has a complete set of hoisting works that was actually used off and on through the 1960s and could be put back into operating condition very easily. (SRH.)

At the Silver Top Mine, a completely intact ore sorting building still remains. This is the only one of its type left in Nevada. The workers assigned to this building suffered tremendously from silicosis because of all of the dust inside. Restoration work has stabilized the building, and it will remain an iconic part of the Tonopah Historic Mining Park for many years to come. (SRH.)

The Silver Top head frame was made from huge redwood timbers hauled in from California. The 1,200-foot shaft is wood lined and is completely intact, in itself a rarity in these old mines. It also has an intact hoist house. These are extremely rare, and for three complete hoisting works to be intact in one place is astonishing. (SRH.)

Two

RHYOLITE AND BULLFROG

Although Rhyolite was relatively short-lived, it has a history of dramatic rise and swift decline. Rhyolite formed soon after Frank "Shorty" Harris and Eddie Cross made rich discoveries in the summer of 1904. Soon a small camp sprang up, called Bullfrog. Another camp, Rhyolite, formed a half mile to the north. One of the first substantial buildings constructed was the $30,000 two-story Southern Hotel.

Rhyolite reached its peak in 1907 and 1908. Its population then was estimated to be anywhere from 8,000 to 12,000. During this time, two weekly newspapers and one daily were published. Rhyolite was served by three railroads, an honor rarely bestowed on any Nevada city.

In January 1907, a network of 400 electric streetlight poles was installed, and soon Rhyolite was brightly lit 24 hours a day. During Rhyolite's brief stardom, more than 85 mining companies were active in the area, with the Montgomery-Shoshone being the most productive.

The financial panic of 1907 killed Rhyolite. The devastating effects of the panic did not reach Rhyolite until 1908. The city emptied as fast as it had been populated only a few years earlier. By the end of 1909, the population was well below 1,000. The Montgomery-Shoshone Mine, the last real hope of survival for Rhyolite, closed after producing close to $2 million.

The population had shrunk to 675 by 1910, and the streetlights were shut off. By 1918, all railroad service had left, but hardly anyone was left to use it for the last few years. The population of the almost-dead town had shrunk to 14 by the beginning of 1920. The last resident, J. D. Lorraine, died in 1924.

Thankfully, for Rhyolite and its visitors, the town site is now under the care of the Bureau of Land Management and the Friends of Rhyolite, working together to preserve what is left of the town and protecting it from further vandalism. Rhyolite is clearly one of the best ghost towns in Nye County and in the state. A visit to Rhyolite in 1979 was the main reason this author embarked on a lifetime of ghost towning.

Rhyolite in May 1905 was a bustling town. The boom is on, and a well-defined street system has already developed after less than a year. As was typical with a fledgling town, the majority of the structures are tents, but at this point, there are already some substantial multiple-story buildings, a sign of the coming prosperity. (CNHS.)

Another early-1905 view of Rhyolite looking to the east shows the town's rapid growth. The town is nestled in a small valley between two mountains. In the distance, a small straight line of white tents is the sister camp of Bullfrog. While the two camps grew separately, within a couple of years, both had grown until they basically merged. (CNHS.)

While the boom was going on in Rhyolite, 5 miles away, Beatty was also growing. The town was centrally located and quickly developed into a shipping center for area mining camps. However, most of its prosperity came from supplying Rhyolite. Here the population of Beatty gathers on Main Street. (CNHS.)

By the summer of 1905, the gap between Bullfrog and Rhyolite was quickly filling in with miners' tents. The town of Bullfrog is comprised of the row of buildings on either side of the wide street to the left. William Stewart's law office is the only wood structure evident in the foreground. (CNHS.)

The bearded gentleman in this photograph is William Stewart. He had served as a senator from Nevada from 1864 until 1875. He was senator again from 1887 until 1905, when he retired. By the time he came to Rhyolite, he was over 80 years old. He practiced law in the booming town until he died in his office on April 23, 1909. (CNHS.)

By December 1905, Rhyolite's population had already grown to about 2,000. The town's main thoroughfare, Golden Street, was lined with business, including some of the first stone buildings constructed. Recreational activities had started, and Rhyolite residents built a baseball field and fielded a team of strong miners. Four different stage lines were running each day to the booming town. (CNHS.)

Frank "Shorty" Harris was already a longtime Nevada and Death Valley prospector when he and Ed Cross made the initial discoveries in the hills above Bullfrog and Rhyolite. Originally from Rhode Island, Harris came west in the 1870s. Most of his adult life was spent in the area. He died at Big Pine, California, and was buried in Death Valley. (CNHS.)

By November 1906, the difference in the scope of Bullfrog has changed. More building has occurred as Rhyolite becomes more crowded and starts extending into Bullfrog. By offering cheaper lots, more businesses began opening here. With the knowledge that the Bullfrog-Goldfield Railroad would have its station here, people had faith that Bullfrog would be a worthy investment. (CNHS.)

Rhyolite continued to grow, with more and more substantial buildings quickly replacing the tents. This view looks north toward Ladd Mountain. During the 1990s and early 21st century, a large open-pit gold mine operated on the back side of the mountain. Today the entire other side has been carved away, but this side remains unchanged. (CNHS.)

The Gold Bar Mine was one of the important early mines in the Rhyolite district. It was located 4 miles northwest of Rhyolite. There was a small camp near the mine. A 10-stamp mill was built in 1907. However, soon after, the financial panic hit and operations ended in 1908. (SRH.)

HOMESTAKE MILL, RHYOLITE, NEV.

The impressive 25-stamp Homestake Mill and Mine were located close to the Gold Bar Mine. A camp of around 50, called Gold Bar, formed below both mines, and most miners lived there. A number of substantial buildings were constructed, but remnants of the camp have disappeared because of later mining. However, the huge foundations of the mill still remain on the hillside. (CNHS.)

The Montgomery-Shoshone Mine was the most productive in Rhyolite. The mine was discovered by a Shoshone Indian who Bob Montgomery had sent to stake a claim for him. Soon afterward, Montgomery sold the mine for a reported $5 million to Charles Schwab, who then built a large 300-ton mill in 1907. The mine was the only one right in Rhyolite and overlooked the town. (SRH.)

At the time Rhyolite reached its peak, the automobile was starting to have its impact. Numerous automobile stage lines were running to Rhyolite from Goldfield and other towns. As long as the autos did not break down, it was faster transportation than the railroads, although the open cars did little to protect from the hot southern Nevada sun. (SS.)

Rhyolite is shown here at its peak in early 1908, before the impact of the financial panic of 1907 had hit. The $50,000 Overbury block and the $90,000 three-story Cook Bank building dominate the skyline. Electric power poles line every street, and the new jail, located at the bottom right, had lots of customers. (CNHS.)

Rhyolite was still in high spirits on the Fourth of July in 1908. Here local firemen participate in a race pulling the hose apparatus. This close-up view gives a great idea of how developed Golden Street was at the town's peak. To the left is the Overbury block and, further down, the white three-storied Cook Bank building. (CNHS.)

As did a number of southern Nevada towns, Rhyolite also had its bottle house. This one contained more than 10,000 bottles. This is one of the few buildings that survive intact in Rhyolite today. It serves as the visitor's center and main office for the Bureau of Land Management. (SS.)

By the 1930s, Rhyolite had been virtually abandoned for 20 years. The difference on Golden Street is dramatic. Almost all of the wood buildings have either been moved elsewhere or torn down for the lumber. The Cook Bank building has already lost its roof, and the other stone buildings are also deteriorated. (CNHS.)

This view of Rhyolite is also from the 1930s. This shows how the once bustling town, crowded with buildings, has been relegated to scattered structures and ruins. The only building that was still occupied was the old Las Vegas and Tonopah Railroad depot, which had been converted into the "Ghost Casino." (CNHS.)

The once proud Cook Bank building stands, but barely. It has had help in its deterioration. During the 1960s, a film company drilled holes in the upper windows to put in Spanish-style railings. Unfortunately, it weakened the structure and led some wall sections to collapse. (SRH.)

The Rhyolite jail is one of only a handful of fully intact buildings left in the town. It still retains all of the steel doors, cells, and bars on the windows. Rhyolite is a wonderful place to visit and explore. However, beware—signs everywhere warn about the rattlesnakes that roam around the site. (SRH.)

The old Las Vegas and Tonopah Railroad depot still retains its stately appearance. Some restoration has taken place already, and the building is fenced off in preparation for resuming the work once funding is found. On special occasions, the building is opened for the public to view. (SRH.)

The Rhyolite-Bullfrog Cemetery is located about a mile south of the old Bullfrog town site. It is rather extensive considering the short lifetime of the town. Numerous old, now unreadable, wood grave markers still remain. The most recent grave dates from 1991 and is of a woman who ran the antique shop in Bullfrog for years. (SRH.)

Three

BELMONT

Belmont is the queen of Nye County ghost towns. Its history began in October 1865 when a Native American discovered a rich deposit of silver, the Highbridge Mine, in the Toquima Mountains. During 1866–1867, Belmont was credited with a population as high as 10,000, but better estimates are about 4,000. Nearby East Belmont also contained a Chinatown. In February 1867, Belmont became the new county seat.

Mining in Belmont's early years was very good. Ten major mines were being worked within a year after the first discoveries. The deepest of these was the 500-foot-deep Belmont Mine. Other important mines were the Monitor-Belmont, Arizona, Combination, Highbridge, and Green and Oder.

Six mills were built in and around Belmont during its peak years. The first was a 10-stamp mill built in 1866, which continued to operate until 1869. In 1867, a larger 20-stamp mill, the Highbridge, was built. The largest mill, the Combination, was completed in February 1868.

The big boom at Gold Mountain, near Bonnie Clare, drained many resources of Belmont beginning in 1880. When the property of the Belmont Mining Company was sold in 1887, Belmont's mining was dead. By 1889, many of the businesses and most of the people had left. From 1865 to 1887, the Belmont mines recorded production in excess of $15 million.

By 1903, Belmont only had 36 qualified voters. In May 1905, Tonopah became the new county seat. Belmont had a fairly active revival beginning in 1914. The Monitor-Belmont Mining Company acquired almost all of the old mines near Belmont and, in August 1915, started the Cameron Mill in East Belmont. The Monitor-Belmont company left the district after closing the Cameron Mill in 1917. The post office closed in 1922, and there have been no revivals since.

In this author's opinion, Belmont is the queen of Nye County ghost towns—in fact, one of the top ghost towns in the state. The remains at and around Belmont are amazing. There are the picturesque ruins of the three mills. Belmont should not be missed.

By 1874, when this overview of Belmont was taken, the town had been in existence for 10 years and served as the Nye County seat. Belmont was at its peak during the mid-1870s with numerous mills and mines in full production. The largest mill was the Combination, a huge 40-stamp mill. (CNHS.)

A view of downtown Belmont during the mid-1870s shows how substantial the town had become. At the far left of the photograph, the Monitor-Belmont Mill is visible. The 20-stamp mill was built in 1867 and was used off and on until the 1910s. Substantial ruins of the mill, including a standing stack, are accessible to visitors. (CNHS.)

The Belmont Court House was easily the most prominent building ever constructed in Belmont. Due to the town's boom, Belmont became the county seat in early 1867. A total of $3,400 was allocated for its construction. The building still stands today and is part of the Nevada State Parks System. (CNHS.)

Education was important in the boom town of Belmont. Numerous schools ran to satisfy the need for knowledge. Here, in 1883, is one of those schools with its entire enrollment in front. The teacher, Charley Deady, stands in the doorway. By 1883, mining activity in Belmont was waning, and all mines had closed by 1887. (CNHS.)

Belmont also had summer school, which surely made students very excited. It is interesting to see the vintage styles of dress students were expected to wear. Here the students and teacher, John Reynolds, pose in 1883 at the George Ernst house. Ernst was a prominent early surveyor and politician for Nye County. His brick house still stands in Belmont. (CNHS.)

Businesses shown along Belmont's main street in 1888 are, from left to right, the Brewery Saloon, Ball and Deady Drug Store (which also housed the post office), a vacant building, and a law office. Looking at the men's dress, one could assume that it was a Sunday morning after services. The Belmont Church was located on a hill overlooking the town. (CNHS.)

All of the Nye County officers gather in this photograph from 1888. Shown are, from left to right, (first row) Henry Ernst (surveyor) and Frank Brotherton (clerk); (second row) George Nichol (commissioner), Adam McClean (treasurer), Andrew Bradley (commissioner), Henry Bohlie (commissioner), and Most Reau (justice of the peace); (third row) Charles Deady (district attorney), John Reynolds (teacher), Charles McGregor (assessor), W. S. Bryden (recorder), Jule Read (deputy sheriff), Wilse Brougher (sheriff), and Bud Smith (deputy sheriff). (CNHS.)

The Andrew Maute home in Belmont, pictured in the 1880s, was typical of the homes of the era. Included in the photograph are, from left to right, (on the porch) Andrew Maute, Louisa Maute, Linda Humphrey, and Daisy Maute; (by the gate) Maggie and Addie Maute and Annie Bradley. Andrew Maute was a newspaper man and owned the *Belmont Courier* from 1876 until it folded in 1901. Unfortunately, this home no longer exists and is only marked by a stone foundation. (CNHS.)

By 1893, Belmont's population had shrunk from a high of 2,000 in 1874 to less than 200. While Belmont still looks like a city this 1893 photograph, the fact was that more than three-quarters of the buildings were already unoccupied. By 1903, Tonopah had taken the county seat and Belmont's population was less than 50. (CNHS.)

This photograph features the home of the McGregor family in upper Belmont in 1901. That is Mrs. McGregor on the right. Her husband, Charles, served as the Nye County assessor. There were no suitable trees in Belmont. Numerous sawmills to the north in the Jefferson area provided lumber for homes and also timber for use in the mines. (CNHS.)

The Cosmopolitan Hotel and Saloon was the most popular place on Main Street in Belmont. Constructed during the boom, it was one of only a few businesses that remained in the town in 1901. The building remained standing until the 1980s, when, in an act of vandalism, the building's main support was pulled out and it collapsed. (CNHS.)

By the time this photograph was taken after Belmont had lost the county seat, many of the buildings have already been razed or moved to other towns and ranches. While Belmont enjoyed a mining revival from 1914 until 1917, it never regained its prominence. Once the revival was over, Belmont became a ghost town. (CNHS.)

This close-up of the Belmont Church, taken in 1901, shows the impact of the years of abandonment. The church was later moved by oxen and flat wagons to Manhattan, where it still stands today. Recently, a replica was built just above the original location and now hosts Sunday services and weddings. (CNHS.)

An interior look at the Combination Mill in 1904 shows just how immense the structure was. Shortly afterward, the mill was dismantled, and the bricks were used to construct the nearby Cameron Mill in 1914. The Combination was a huge investment, costing $225,000 to build. At the time, it was one of the most impressive mills in central Nevada. (CNHS.)

This is the exterior of the Combination Mill shortly before its dismantlement. The size of the mill was incredible, covering most of the hillside. Immense foundations still remain, as does the smokestack at the right of the photograph. This is the only known photograph showing the Combination Mill. (CNHS.)

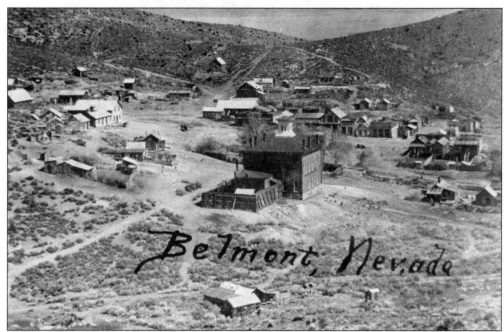

A view of Belmont from 1905, looking east, shows the deterioration of the town. Many buildings have disappeared, and there is little life on the streets. Attached to the rear of the courthouse is the jail. The cells were torn out in the 1930s and used in the new Gabbs jail. Recently, the cells were returned when the Gabbs jail was torn down. The cells are part of the ongoing restoration efforts at the courthouse. (CNHS.)

This 1904 view of the abandoned Monitor Belmont Mill shows the now quiet mill. The 20-stamp mill had been built in 1867 by the Belmont Silver Mining Company. The mill closed in the 1880s but was reactivated during the revival that began in 1914. Ruins of the mill are located about a half mile south of downtown Belmont. (CNHS.)

By the 1930s, only a couple of people still lived in Belmont. The windows are gone from the courthouse, which was then used as a hay barn. Most of the hundreds of buildings are gone, and even the business district on Main Street is mostly gone. The brick Ernst home still stands at the lower end of the trees. (CNHS.)

The Cosmopolitan was still standing when the author took this photograph in the early 1980s. The purposeful destruction of the building is a true historical travesty. The Central Nevada Museum had just received grant funding for stabilizing and restoring the building when the incident took place. The sign and post office boxes were saved and are in the courthouse. (SRH.)

Belmont has one of the most interesting cemeteries of any ghost town. A wide variety of styles exist, including this one with its ornate wrought iron. Local residents recently undertook a complete restoration of the cemetery, including building a new entrance, fencing the cemetery, and restoration of the graves. (SRH.)

The original stone office building for the Combination Silver Mining Company has recently been restored and converted into a bed-and-breakfast. It offers visitors a unique opportunity to get a good taste of the Old West and spend some time enjoying the wonderful sights that Belmont offers. (SRH.)

In East Belmont, located 2 miles east of Belmont, numerous 1860s-era stone miners' cabins are left. Made from local stone, each cabin ruin features a unique style of fireplace. These are located between the ruins of the Cameron and Combination Mills. More than 20 cabins are scattered in that area. (SRH.)

Only the brick shell of the Cameron Mill remains. After the mill shut down in the late 1910s, all of the milling equipment was removed and sold. The mainstays of Belmont, the silver mines, are located behind the mill ruins. East Belmont is actually the oldest section of Belmont and where the first residents lived. (SRH.)

The foundation and stack of the Combination Mill dominate the ruins of East Belmont. The stack has a unique story. The damage at the top of the stack is from military aircraft. Jets would use the stack for target practice while traveling between Fallon Naval Air Station and Nellis Air Force Base. Despite this, the tall stack is still structurally solid. (SRH.)

Four

MANHATTAN

The Manhattan district was active long before the town of Manhattan even formed. George Nicholl discovered rich silver ore in 1866. By 1869, activity slowed, and by the beginning of winter, the district was totally abandoned. In April 1905, a new discovery was made by cowpuncher John Humphrey from Big Smoky Valley. With this discovery, Manhattan literally sprang up.

The San Francisco earthquake of April 1906 jolted Manhattan almost as much as it did San Francisco. The population quickly dropped to a few hundred. New discoveries in September 1906 and June 1907 kept the town barely alive. The town's perseverance paid off when, in 1909, rich placer deposits were discovered a few miles below Manhattan. The town also received the first wireless telegraph in Nevada. The discovery revitalized the town to some extent.

Activity was boosted again in 1912 when a rich new lode was discovered at the bottom of the already rich White Caps Mine. The population of Manhattan rose to almost 1,000 during the next two years. After the 1920s, production declined and most operations shut down.

The 1920s were a slow mining period for Manhattan, and two devastating fires destroyed most of downtown. On December 23, 1920, a fire that started in the Pine Tree Garage and Bank Saloon burned over 30 businesses. Another fire in May 1922 burned the south side of the business district. Another fire, one week later, burned the Victoria Hotel and more of the business district. In addition, the two May fires burned almost 50 homes. Only some of the businesses and homes were ever rebuilt.

Total production of the Manhattan district is well over $12 million. After dredging operations ceased in 1947, Manhattan began once more to slip into ghost town status. During the 1980s, new mining activity took place near Manhattan. A new underground mine recently started operations. The town still has a population of 50, and the post office and saloons remain open. The remains at Manhattan are extensive and very interesting. A visit to the Manhattan Cemetery, located half a mile west of town, is a must.

While Manhattan was first discovered in 1866 and had modest production until 1869, little was built. The true boom began in 1905, and very quickly, businesses began opening on Main Street. The freight wagons and unloaded lumber show a new town bustling with life. The Manhattan Post Office opened on Christmas 1905. (CNHS.)

A view of Manhattan in early 1906, looking east, shows the rapid growth of the town. Already, a number of two-story buildings have been constructed along Main Street. The boom was tempered by tragedy. The town's sheriff, Thomas Logan, was murdered in April 1906. The accused murderer was eventually acquitted despite numerous eyewitnesses. (CNHS.)

The Austin–Manhattan stage comes flying into Manhattan during the spring of 1906. Because of its remoteness, Manhattan required service from stage and freight lines in all directions to meet its needs. The booming town was even bestowed with a Wells Fargo express office, which only served the most promising and richer mining camps. (CNHS.)

This is a 1906 view of Manhattan during its boom, looking west. This shows that while development along Main Street progressed rapidly, many residents were still living in tents. Once the summer came and the snow melted, many finally had the chance to build more substantial housing. (CNHS.)

A close-up view of Main Street Manhattan in the spring of 1906 features some of the prominent buildings. The two-story Merchant's Hotel dominates the skyline. Large stacked piles of lumber show that businessmen were preparing to do extensive construction once the weather warmed up. By the summer of 1906, more than 2,000 people were living in the town. (CNHS.)

The year 1906 also saw the opening of the first school in Manhattan. When it opened, it had 16 students. The next year, there were almost 100. Soon a new stone-and-masonry school opened to accommodate more students. The school still stands and has been used as the Manhattan Public Library for years. (CNHS.)

This is a spring 1907 close-up view of the Merchant's Hotel, which was the most impressive in Manhattan and featured amenities rare in hotels of the period: indoor plumbing, electric lights, and a Western Union office. Note the muddy street. Manhattan was notorious for its muddy streets during the spring and flash floods in the summer. (CNHS.)

By early 1908, Manhattan's main street was wall-to-wall businesses. Here a 14-horse freight team brings in a large load of supplies. At its peak, Manhattan was served by no less than a dozen stage and freight lines, which led to considerable congestion. Slowly, the advent of the automobile took over. (CNHS.)

A number of the mines were located in the mountains above Manhattan. This made hauling the ore to the mills a challenge. Here two wagons are loaded at one of the many large ore bins. Since it was all downhill to the town, the drivers had their hands full trying to keep the heavy wagons from getting away from them. (CNHS.)

Winter and spring always made Manhattan's streets a mess. By 1907, when this photograph was taken, the automobile had already made an appearance. Manhattan boasted one of the earlier dealerships in the state. An auto stage ran between Tonopah and Manhattan for many years and led to the closing of the horse stage lines. (CNHS.)

By 1910, most of the Manhattan district had been claimed and mines sprang up everywhere. Because of the richness of the ore, many claims were subdivided, leading to mines whose property was not much bigger than the shaft itself. This photograph of the hills to the west of Manhattan perfectly shows that. (CNHS.)

A miner in the White Caps Mine works on drilling a raise at the 165-foot level during 1912. Underground mining was a dangerous venture for even the most experienced miners. Most mining deaths in the old days were from collapsing tunnels. Drilling overhead led to slabs of rock breaking loose and falling down, crushing the miners. A new strike in this mine during 1912 led to a revival in the town. After a slowdown of a couple years, the population rose to more than 2,000 residents by the end of the year. (CNHS.)

By 1917, a new mill had been built at the White Caps Mine, and production continued until 1940. The mine was the richest and most productive of all of Manhattan's mines, producing $2.7 million in gold and silver. The mill later burned down. There are plans to once again reopen the mine. (CNHS.)

This is a 1913 view of the Big Four Mine and Mill in Manhattan. The company was quite successful and profitable. It was highly cost effective for them to have the mine directly attached to the mill, eliminating the need to ship ore for treatment. However, the high-grade ore only lasted for a couple of years. (SRH.)

The mine and mill of the Manhattan Milling and Ore Company are pictured during the 1920s. This company and the White Caps company were the mainstays of Manhattan's production through the 1920s while other companies were folding. The two companies were involved in many years of litigation over claims before they were resolved in 1917. (CNHS.)

The War Eagle Mill of the Associated Milling Company is seen in 1908, soon after its completion. The impressive mill operated at full capacity for a number of years, but after mining slowed in the early 1910s, its usefulness was gone. A five-stamp battery from the ruins was salvaged in the 1990s and installed at the Tonopah Historic Mining Park. (CNHS.)

The main street in Manhattan was still a fairly busy place in 1915. The town's population hovered around 1,000 despite the slowdown in mining fortunes. A new schoolhouse had just been built, which was used until 1955. During this period, it was primarily the White Caps Mine that was keeping Manhattan alive. (CNHS.)

This view of Manhattan was taken in 1915 from Gold Hill. The buildings are primarily wood, although some, like the Nye and Ormsby Bank, were made from native stone. Virtually all of the white miners' tents have been replaced by small wood cabins. By this point, most of the usable wood had been stripped from the hillsides overlooking the town. (CNHS.)

Another 1915 view of Manhattan was taken from Mustang Hill. The white church in the center is the original one from Belmont that was moved by horse a few years earlier. At this time, while still a vibrant town, Manhattan had already reached its peak and was slowly losing its residents. (CNHS.)

In 1910, because of the high demand for electricity for the mines and town, the Nevada-California Power Company built this substantial concrete substation at the lower end of the town. In the 1970s, it was sold and used as an antique and curio shop until it was torn down in the 1990s to make way for a new open-pit gold mine. (CNHS.)

Placer gold had been discovered in 1909, but in 1939, placer mining became serious with the installation of a 3,000-ton dredge. The dredge was owned by the Manhattan Gold Dredging Company. It was floated by making ponds on the gold areas. It operated until 1946 and produced over $4.6 million in gold. (CNHS.)

In this overview of the placer mining area of Manhattan in the early 1940s, the town is located to the east and its lowest buildings can be seen at the end of the gravel road. The large barren area along the road is the first section of gravel processed by the huge dredge. The Manhattan Mill, although idle for many years, is still intact. The power substation is to the right. (CNHS.)

The day shift at the White Caps Mine poses at the mine shaft in the 1940s. At the time, it was the only producing mine in the district. The mine closed down in 1946, although occasionally attempts were made to reopen it and start production, with little success. Once the mine closed, the mines in Manhattan were quiet until 1980. (CNHS.)

Looking down Main Street during the 1940s, it was clear that Manhattan's glory days were gone. Only a couple dozen people still called the town home. The once proud buildings along the street have already begun to deteriorate. Despite this, the Manhattan Post Office still remains open to this day. (CNHS.)

Despite years of neglect and harsh weather, the remains of the mine manager's home at the White Caps Mine still stand. The mine is located high above Manhattan, about 2 miles to the southeast. Since it was the largest mine in the district, a substantial complex of buildings, including some housing, was constructed at the mine. It makes for interesting exploring. (SRH.)

One of the original machine shops still struggles to stand at the White Caps. Many buildings still remain at the site, albeit in various stages of decay. Just over the building, the huge metal smelter of the mill is visible. Some mining work is going on right now, but none of the original structures have been disturbed. (SRH.)

Not much is keeping this building standing at White Caps. This is the on-site mining office for the White Caps Mining Company. It is located on a ridge that overlooks the mine and mill area, which allowed the officers a great viewing area to keep an eye on the work site. (SRH.)

An overview of the White Caps Mine complex exhibits that much is left. The huge shaft of the mine is located just out of the picture to the right. All that remains of the mill is the large crusher/smelter. All the superstructure of the mill was destroyed in a fire many years ago. White Caps must be visited when at Manhattan. (SRH.)

Five

TYBO

Original discoveries were made in the Hot Creek range in 1866. The first major ore discovery in Tybo was made in 1870 by Dr. Galley and M. V. Gillett. The discovery was later developed into the Two-G Mine. It was not until 1874 that a small camp began to form in Tybo Canyon. A small lead smelter was built in the canyon in 1874, and in the next year, the Tybo Consolidated Mining Company formed.

By the summer of 1876, the small town had boomed to a population of almost 1,000. Buildings in the town in 1876 included five stores, a number of saloons, two blacksmith shops, and a post office. Tybo was basically a company town of the Tybo Consolidated Mining Company. From 1877 to 1880, Tybo was the top producer of Nye County and second only to Eureka in total lead production. The Tybo Consolidated Mining Company ran into problems and folded in 1881, when the quality of the ore dropped drastically. By the end of 1881, only 100 people were left in Tybo Canyon. During the next 25 years, Tybo barely managed to cling to life.

Tybo was given another lease on life when the Louisiana Consolidated Mining Company began to work the mines in 1916. The company brought electricity and telegraph and telephone service to the town in March 1920. The company left the district in 1937. Soon Tybo was emptied again, with only rows of deserted, decaying buildings acknowledging that people had ever been here.

The last revival at Tybo started in 1926 when the Treadwell Yukon Company, Ltd., began operations. By the end of 1929, some 180 men were on the payroll, and Tybo's population had grown to 228 by 1930. The revival ended in 1937 when the company closed. From 1929 to 1937, $6.8 million was produced. Total production for the Tybo district is $9.8 million.

Even today, Tybo is not a complete ghost. A handful of people still make their home in the peaceful, beautiful canyon. Tybo is one of the better ghost towns in Nye County. Extensive mines, charcoal kilns, and mill ruins are scattered throughout the canyon.

While silver was discovered at Tybo in 1866, the town did not form until 1874, after a rich lode was found. By the time this photograph was taken in 1875, Tybo already had the look of an established town. By 1876, Tybo had a population of 1,000 and continued to grow. (CNHS.)

The impressive 20-stamp mill and smelter of the Tybo Consolidated Mining Company began operations in August 1874. The company controlled the three major mines at Tybo: Casket, Lafayette, and the Two-G. The town was basically a company town. (CNHS.)

A number of other mines were active during the 1870s besides those of the Tybo Consolidated Mining Company. This mine is located about a mile above the town site in an area known as Upper Tybo. The cabin in the foreground still stands today. (CNHS.)

At nearby Hot Creek, a fancy hotel was built. The small town was a center for stage and freight lines. Most supplies for Tybo came through Hot Creek via Eureka to the north. With its hot springs and hotel, many Tybo residents made weekend recreational trips here. (CNHS.)

By 1876, Tybo boasted five stores, numerous saloons, two blacksmith shops, and a post office. The Trowbridge Store was one of the first to open and, many years later, ended up being the last business to close. Note the large stack of filled ore bags awaiting shipment to Eureka. (CNHS.)

The Bunker Hill Mine, shown in the foreground, was a prominent producer when photographed in 1875. This was the section known as Upper Tybo. It was comprised of the primary miners' cabins. The main town of Tybo starts at the end of the visible canyon, to the west. (CNHS.)

The Two-G Mine was the mainstay throughout Tybo's mining history. It was the richest and largest in the district. It was located just above the town. In the far background, the Tybo Consolidated Company's mill is visible just above the white company office building in the center. (CNHS.)

The large 20-stamp mill and smelter of the Tybo Consolidated Company were still under construction when photographed in 1875. Because of the amount of ore needing treatment, a new mill had to be built to replace a smaller smelter constructed in 1874. The mill was active until 1880. (CNHS.)

Not much activity took place in Tybo after 1881 until the Treadwell Yukon Company took control of the area's claims and began a major operation mining lead. The company built this 350-ton concentration mill and smelter in 1929. This new activity brought back about 75 residents to Tybo, which had been a virtual ghost town for almost 50 years. (CNHS.)

With the arrival of an army of miners, the Treadwell Company had to provide accommodations since the old buildings left from Tybo's early days were not suitable. A large three-story boardinghouse was constructed along with a separate kitchen building. The company took good care of its workers, opening a number of businesses to cater to their needs. (CNHS.)

With the company employing almost 200 men, Tybo's population rose to close to 300 by 1930. With the Depression ongoing, employees were very loyal and job turnover was next to nothing. All of the buildings visible here were built by the company. The mine and mill are located on the mountain to the left. (CNHS.)

After a long day, miners head to the "mess hall" of the Treadwell Company. This was also the recreation building for the workers, having pool tables, a newsstand, and other amenities. It was located just to the left of one of the dormitories. To the left is the brick Trowbridge Store. (CNHS.)

In addition to all of the housing constructed for miners, the company also built so-called "executive" housing. These were used by the company's on-site managers and supervisors. One was kept ready as a guesthouse for visiting VIPs. None of these buildings remain today. (CNHS.)

A 1934 overview of the Treadwell-Yukon operation shows just how large the mining and milling complex was. However, it was a simple and efficient operation. Ore came right out of the mine and, using a gravity process, was fed directly into the mill. Once processing was completed, the ore was loaded directly into ore trucks for shipment. (CNHS.)

During 1932, a fleet of tandem ore trucks prepares for the 70-mile trip to Tonopah. The concentrate was hauled to Millers, 10 miles west of Tonopah, where processing into silver and gold bars was completed. Each truck could haul 28 tons of lead concentrate, and each round-trip took almost all day. (CNHS.)

By 1934, operations at Tybo were still robust despite the unfavorable economic climate in the nation. However, the ore values in the mine had started to decline, signaling trouble for the future. To compound the problem, the price for a pound of lead also began a steady drop. (CNHS.)

Here is a close-up of the main shaft of the Treadwell Yukon Company in 1939 after operations had ceased. The entire operation was shut down in 1937, bringing an end to Tybo's long history. During its years, the company produced $6.8 million in lead. The town was completely abandoned shortly after and has been a ghost town ever since. (CNHS.)

The ruins of the schoolhouse still stand. Recently, a local landowner undertook a personal project and has worked on restoring the building. A new roof has been installed and structure repair work done. It is always rewarding to see people taking such projects on to help preserve the vanishing history. (SRH.)

Tybo is well-known for its many existing charcoal kilns that are scattered in a number of nearby canyons. These stone kilns are located a couple of miles above the Tybo town site. Built in 1874, they were the first kilns around Tybo. The charcoal was needed to smelt the silver out of the difficult ore. (SRH.)

These are the ruins of the Tybo Consolidated Mill. The massive concrete foundations dominate the town site. This view shows the upper part of the foundations. The vertical line of stones was actually an in-ground chimney from the lower smelter section. It rose up to the concrete form at the top, where the smokestack stood. (SRH.)

The Tybo Cemetery provides some wonderful photographic opportunities. Some fancy fencing, like this, wood headboards, and marble headstones remain. However, more than three-quarters of the graves are unmarked. Unfortunately, many of these remote cemeteries never had any records made and the names are lost to history forever. (SRH.)

Five

GOLDFIELD

Goldfield was the scene of the last true American gold rush. From nothing but sagebrush and sand, a town that would reach a peak population in excess of 20,000 sprang to life. All it took was one of the richest gold districts ever to make it happen. The first discoveries took place during the fall of 1902 by Tom Fisherman, Billy Marsh, and Harry Stimler. During 1903, claims were developed, and by the spring of 1904, a full-scale gold rush had started. Within a few months, more than 4,000 people had flocked to the town.

The next few years were a time of incredible growth. Hundreds of businesses were built, numerous mines began producing millions in gold, huge mills were constructed, three railroads began service to Goldfield, and an epic championship boxing match was held. It was also the scene of the most intense labor disputes in Nevada history between the rival Western Federation of Mines and the Industrial Workers of the World. That culminated with federal troops having to be brought in during December 1907.

By 1908, most of the high-producing mines were under the control of the Goldfield Consolidated Mining Company. Production from the mines peaked in 1910, but ore values became lower and major mining ceased in 1918 when the Goldfield Consolidated Company closed down. Some small production periods have taken place since but nothing approaching the glory years.

Goldfield has had its struggles but still has a population of around 300 today and maintains its status as the county seat for Esmeralda County; it still has many impressive buildings, including the Goldfield Hotel, courthouse, and bank building. The original two-story firehouse has been recently restored and houses a museum. Every year, the town sponsors Goldfield Days in August, which features a land auction and many activities, including tours of the historic sites in town. Remnants of its rich mining history abound throughout the area with old wood head frames, mill ruins, and other mining artifacts scattered everywhere. The town has an active restoration program, which has already restored many historic places.

The first discoveries at Goldfield were made in the fall of 1902. Word spread and people began arriving during the spring of 1903. By 1904, one of the United States' last gold rushes was underway. This photograph, taken during the spring, shows some of the first arrivals. Only tents were evident, but substantial buildings would soon be constructed. (CNHS.)

By September 1904, Goldfield had developed dramatically and already had a population of a few thousand. This photograph was taken at the corner of Main Street and Mayers Street. Buildings were being constructed as fast as lumber could be hauled in. One of the first brick buildings in Goldfield is under construction to the right. (CNHS.)

Freight lines were the lifeblood of early Goldfield. Everything had to be hauled to the rapidly growing town. This, however, was a rather unique load. In August 1904, the first car in Goldfield was hauled in. It was a 16-horsepower Rambler that was used by "Alkali Bill" Brong on an auto stage. (CNHS.)

Main Street of Goldfield was undergoing rapid transformation as buildings were being constructed constantly. After a land auction, virtually all of the property along the street had been sold and every owner hurried to get their business going to take advantage of the tremendous demand for goods of all kinds. (CNHS.)

83

This is another view of Main Street looking in the opposite direction, taken later in 1904. The two-story hotel on the left is the same as in the previous photograph on the right. Since the other photograph was taken, the hotel has been completed and a veranda added. The incredible growth rate of Goldfield continued for a number of years before peaking. (CNHS.)

Main Street stretched for over a mile, and by the end of 1904, hundreds of businesses lined the street, with the side streets also rapidly filling up. Goods were arriving so rapidly that, as seen here, they were just unloaded right in the street until the items could be brought into the buildings when they were completed. (CNHS.)

Enterprising businessmen tapped into the incredible demand for building materials. Wood was not available locally and was expensive to have hauled in. Here adobe bricks are being made just south of Goldfield. Buildings made of adobe bricks provided better protection during the cold winters and kept the homes cooler during the hot summers. (CNHS.)

The auto stages operating in Goldfield were also used for recreational trips. The favorite place was Alkali Springs, located about 10 miles northwest of Goldfield. These hot springs were the scene of much activity. A fancy restaurant was built there, and a huge spa was developed that hosted picnics, dances, and parties until the late 1910s. (CNHS.)

A large freight team brings another load of building lumber into Goldfield from Tonopah during 1905. The freight lines were trying to capitalize on business quickly because, at this time, the railroad was being built and would arrive in September. Once the railroad arrived, business for the horse-hauled freight lines dropped dramatically since deliveries were mostly hauled by rail. (CNHS.)

Looking southwest from Main and Crook Streets during late 1905, one can see how extensive development has been. A number of multistory stone and adobe-brick buildings have already been completed. The town's red light district was located at the far end of the street, and a brewery is already in operation at the foot of the hill in the background. (CNHS.)

A close-up shows the Mohawk Mine, one of the many rich mines that help to cement Goldfield's rich legacy. The Mohawk was owned by the Goldfield Consolidated Mining Company, the richest company in the district. The production of the mines peaked in 1910 when more than $10.7 million in gold was mined. (CNHS.)

Because of the large amount of ore being produced from the Goldfield Consolidated Mining Company's mines, the company began construction of what would be the largest mill ever built in Goldfield. The mill had 100 stamps, an unusually high amount. Once the mill was completed, the rich ore paid for the construction costs within six months. (Nevada State Museum.)

A huge celebration was held in Goldfield during September 1905 when the last spike was driven into the Tonopah and Goldfield Railroad terminus. This signaled a dramatic shift in the fortunes of the town and showed Goldfield had established itself and would remain a prominent town for many years. (CNHS.)

Despite the fact that Goldfield had sprung up in the middle of the desert, there were some big amenities that surprisingly were available in the town. A large dairy farm was established on the outskirts of Goldfield, and daily delivery service was established. Here a Sanitary Dairy milk wagon delivers milk in the residential section during 1906. (CNHS.)

Boxing matches became the vogue of entertainment in Goldfield. A world championship match between the reigning champion, Joe Gans, and Oscar "Battling" Nelson was held on August 11, 1906. Here Nelson arrives in Goldfield. The fight was promoted by local resident George "Tex" Rickard, who later became famous for building Madison Square Garden. (CNHS.)

Nelson (left) and Gans (right) meet at the center of the ring before beginning their epic battle. It was an extremely hot day for the fight, scheduled for 45 rounds. It was a seesaw affair that saw Gans break his hand in the 33rd round. Nelson had been constantly warned about his fouls, and a particularly blatant one in the 42nd disqualified him; Gans was declared the winner. (Nevada State Museum.)

Goldfield pulled out all the stops to prepare for the Gans-Nelson fight. An impressive purse of $33,500 was amassed, although the champion Gans was only to get $11,000. The gate receipt was $76,000, a record for boxing at that time. There were 6,200 fight fans who filled the specially built arena to capacity. (CNHS.)

By 1907, Goldfield had become quite a railroad town, being served by the Tonopah and Goldfield, Bullfrog and Goldfield, and Las Vegas and Tonopah Railroads. This view is of the Tonopah and Goldfield Railroad yard, located on the east side of Goldfield, with the depot to the right. The buildings and rails are all gone now. (CNHS.)

The Las Vegas and Tonopah Railroad passenger depot in Goldfield was an impressive structure in 1908. This railroad was the first to stop service to Goldfield in the 1910s, but the railroad depot survived for many years. However, time finally won, and the building was taken down a number of years ago. Only the foundation remains. (CNHS.)

Las Vegas and Tonopah Railroad engine No. 5 was one of many engines used. The line ran through other boom towns such as Pioneer, Rhyolite, and Beatty on its way to Las Vegas. While a major player in southern Nevada history, the company was badly managed, which led to its short run. (CNHS.)

An overview shows the Florence Mine and Mill in 1907, shortly after the construction of its new mill. The Florence was one of the most productive mines in Goldfield's history. Even today, some limited mining takes place in the deep shaft. During its peak, the mine was producing $10,000 a day in gold. While the mill was dismantled years ago, the mine head frame still stands, proudly overlooking Goldfield. (CNHS.)

92

During 1907, the mighty Goldfield Hotel was built. It was one of the most modern hotels in the West, offering a fancy restaurant, running hot water, modern plumbing, and electric elevators. A number of other attractive stone buildings are being constructed adjacent to it. However, a major fire later in 1923 destroyed 53 blocks of the city. The hotel survived, but almost all the other buildings in the photograph were burned. (CNHS.)

A fine two-story firehouse was built to serve Goldfield. Here the firefighters and two of their pumper wagons pose in front of the new station in 1908. Despite having to protect a city that had an estimated peak population of more than 30,000, the men performed many heroic feats to save buildings and people. By the time the huge fire of 1923 destroyed most of the town, the department had been pretty much disbanded. (CNHS.)

To better serve the local mines, the railroads built spurs to the mines with which they had hauling contracts. Here, in 1908, a Las Vegas and Tonopah Railroad train loads up with ore from the huge bin of the Mohawk Mine, part of the Goldfield Consolidated Mining Company's holdings. By the time the company shut down in 1918, the mines of the Goldfield district had produced more than $80 million. (CNHS.)

Because of the shape of the area where Goldfield was established, the town was prone to flash floods throughout its history. The flood shown here on September 13, 1913, was the most infamous. Many businesses and homes were destroyed by the high waters. Numerous homes in the residential section were completely swept away and ended up in the valley below Goldfield. (CNHS.)

By 1940, very few businesses were still open in Goldfield. After all of the major mining had ended around 1920, the town continued losing population. Only about 1,000 were left by 1940. The hotel had been closed, but during World War II, it was reopened mainly to accommodate the large number of troops heading off to war. The Tonopah and Goldfield Railroad was mandated to remain in operation by the government. After the war, both shut down for good. (CNHS.)

Today many buildings still remain in Goldfield. The town is still the county seat for Esmeralda County. Even though it only has 300 residents, it is the largest town in the county. Most of the old remaining structures survived the 1923 fire because they were made of stone or adobe. This structure is one of the lucky few wood buildings to survive. (SRH.)

The Florence Mine is still being actively worked, although on a small scale. A more recent mill has been constructed adjacent to the mine to prepare ore for shipment. A number of the old head frames remain and are scattered around the outskirts of Goldfield. The huge foundations of the Goldfield Consolidated mill are located just to the north of town. (SRH.)

The old school struggles to stand in modern Goldfield. It has been abandoned for years, but there are ongoing efforts to raise restoration funds. The community takes its history very seriously, and a number of wonderful restorations, including the old firehouse, have already been completed. It is hoped that the new owners of the Goldfield Hotel will begin restoring that building. (SRH.)

Seven

CANDELARIA

For a Nevada mining town, Candelaria had a relatively long existence. The first discoveries were made as early as 1863, although it was not until 10 years later that the deposits were developed. The first mine, the Northern Belle, became the mainstay of production for Candelaria throughout its history. A boom began in 1873 that saw rapid development near the Northern Belle in Pickhandle Gulch, located above the future site of Candelaria. The actual Candelaria town site was not organized until the summer of 1876 but grew rapidly afterward. Within a month, the town had two hotels, a post office, and, of course, many saloons.

Because of easier access to water, two large mills were constructed at nearby Belleville, about 9 miles away. For more than 10 years in a row, silver production from Candelaria was more than $1 million a year. The best years for the town were from 1881 to 1883, when Candelaria's population was close to 2,000. However, the town gained a reputation for violence and was considered by many to be the toughest camp in Nevada.

A big boost to the town was the arrival of the Carson and Colorado Railroad in early 1882. However, it arrived toward the end of Candelaria's prosperity. A devastating miners' strike during the summer of 1885 spelled the end of the town. Within a year, the town was virtually empty. Short revivals took place in 1890 and 1919 but never brought any life back to the town. The town has essentially been empty for more than 120 years, and not much has survived those tough desert years.

Beginning in 1980, a new microscopic open-pit operation began work. A number of different companies continued to work the pits until the early 21st century. As many as 200 men were employed at peak times during the years, and more than 30 million ounces of silver were produced. During the operations, most of the remains in Pickhandle Gulch were destroyed. At Candelaria, numerous stone ruins and a cemetery still remain. This is a wonderful ghost town to spend time exploring.

By 1875, a small camp had formed in Pickhandle Gulch, which was named Metallic City. The actual town of Candelaria was not organized until August 1876. Until then, Columbus had served as a surrogate town. In 1888, a man named James Casey was born here. Later, after working in the freighting business in Candelaria, he would move to Seattle and start the American Messenger Company, which later became UPS. (CNHS.)

This is a rare late-1876 overview of the new town of Candelaria. Barely three months after the town was established, Candelaria's rapid growth is evident in this photograph. This was in spite of the exorbitant cost of having materials shipped from the nearest shipping point near Reno, more than 100 miles away. (Southerland Studios.)

The Northern Belle Mine was well developed by the time this photograph was taken in 1876. While the original mines up in Pickhandle Gulch were still working, it was the Northern Belle that was by far the main producer of silver. The buildings in the lower left corner are part of the residential section of Candelaria, showing how close the mine was to town. (CNHS.)

Up in Pickhandle Gulch, the Columbus Consolidated Mine had a well-established mine complex, complete with housing for its workers. The house to the right served as the mine superintendent's residence. The two longer buildings are dormitories for workers. The mine had its own crushing mill, and ore was fed down to the storage bin for pickup. (CNHS.)

By 1885, the Columbus Consolidated Mine camp had expanded even further. In this close-up, a number of new buildings have been constructed, including the small false-front saloon and a mercantile store in the lower right. Visible next to the mine dump are the new offices for the mining company. (CNHS.)

By the time this overview of Candelaria was taken in 1887, the town was in serious decline. While the main street still boasts many substantial buildings, most were already abandoned. The Northern Belle Mine and Mill, to the upper left, had shut down the year before. It is interesting to note that the streets are completely empty. (CNHS.)

This is an 1887 close-up view of the surface works at the Mount Diablo Mine, one of the main producers. The Northern Belle is adjacent to the property to the left. The Carson and Colorado Railroad has run a spur by the two mines to easily transfer the ore for shipment to the mills at Belleville. As is evident by the lack of activity and no smoke from the stack, the property had already shut down as a result of Candelaria's decline. (CNHS.)

The few remaining residents of Candelaria gather in the still-open Nevada Hotel on Main Street in 1887. People held out hope for the town to revive, and their hopes were answered when the mines were reopened in 1890. This activity did bring a few hundred residents back to the town until the mines closed again in 1892. (CNHS.)

A panoramic view of Candelaria taken in 1888 shows the town and adjacent mines. The photograph is taken from the mine dump of the Mount Diablo Mine. The Northern Belle is visible to the

By the time this photograph was taken in 1893, Candelaria was at the tail end of its revival. This short rebirth brought workers back to town. Having home delivery was a special amenity. Swain and Ingalls Delivery Company was one that provided that service. Here Otis and W. A. Ingalls make a delivery up in Pickhandle Gulch. (CNHS.)

right. The buildings in the center background mark the entrance to Pickhandle Gulch, where a number of residents chose to reside. (CNHS.)

This 1895 view of downtown Candelaria was taken from the lawn of the Mount Diablo Mine owner's large house. By this time, the revival had ended and the town was already on its way back to being a ghost town. The level of activity on Main Street is noticeably extremely low. The train tended to be full leaving town and empty coming in. (CNHS.)

Candelaria had a number of schools over the years. Here all 28 students in grades 1 through 12 gather at the front of the school. The teacher at the time was Miss Starling. At its peak, Candelaria had three schools and more than 100 students. Students living in Belleville came over to the town on the train. (CNHS.)

The Carson and Colorado Railroad depot at Candelaria was still open during the early-1890s revival. Only a few days after the celebration of the first train in town on February 29, 1882, a large gust of wind blew the depot over and it rolled down the hill. It was replaced but was carefully anchored down this time. (CNHS.)

By 1900, only a few hardy residents still occupied Candelaria. This view is up Main Street, and the fancy home at the end of the street is the house from which the previous photograph was taken five years earlier. The idle Mount Diablo Mine and Mill are in the background. (CNHS.)

While little mining activity was taking place, by 1900, there were still some residents in the town and enough ore being produced to keep the train running and freight wagons hauling. During this period, the post office also remained open. Here a 22-horse team hauls freight from the Chiatovich Ranch in Little Fish Lake Valley. (CNHS.)

Over the years, while major activity had ceased, the mines around Candelaria were still occasionally opened and run on a small scale. In 1955, the Northern Belle, shown here, was a minor producer. The ore bin and mine were refurbished, although the old railroad tracks are noticeably gone by this time. (CNHS.)

By 1955, the once proud Mount Diablo Mill had been dismantled and only the boiler and smokestack were left behind. Unfortunately, when old mills were abandoned, this was normally their final fate. Typically, the superstructure would be ripped down to allow easier access to remove the valuable milling equipment. (CNHS.)

The remnants of two 20-stamp mills dominate the ruins of Belleville, a milling suburb of Candelaria. The impressive cut-stone walls are extensive and huge. The mills were built in 1873 and 1876, and the town had a population as high as 600. After a water pipeline to Candelaria was completed in 1882, new mills built there eliminated the need for Belleville, and it was abandoned soon after. (SRH.)

Only the concrete foundations remain of this relic of Candelaria's early history. With all of the activity during the 1990s and the next decade, very little remains of the town's mining history. The head frame of the Northern Belle Mine, however, was rescued, has been restored, and is at a museum in Tonopah. (SRH.)

The solid stone front of an old mercantile store is all that is left, the rest having collapsed over the many years of abandonment. All of the stone used in Candelaria's buildings was mined locally, which made stone much more affordable than the cost of having lumber shipped many miles. (SRH.)

The old bank building still retains one of its steel doors, and its large safe is under the rubble of the collapsed roof. The door is wide open but gives a wonderful sense of what a bank looked like back in the 1880s. This is one of the most complete buildings left in the town. However, the extensive ruins at the town and mines, and the cemetery, make Candelaria a great place to explore. (SRH.)

Eight

CARRARA

Initial activity in the Carrara area in 1904 indicated some very promising marble outcroppings, but they turned out to be too fractured to be saleable. In 1911, new deposits were found that were not as fractured, and the American Carrara Marble Company was formed. The quarry was located in the mountains. The town of Carrara grew next to the Las Vegas and Tonopah Railroad, about 3 miles from the quarry. Because of the distance from the quarry to the LV&T, work on a 3-mile spur line was started during 1913.

"Townsite Day" was celebrated on May 8, 1913, to officially dedicate the town. Some buildings were moved to Carrara from Beatty and Rhyolite to help the town look more completed than it really was. Townsite Day was a gala celebration and included a band from Goldfield and a baseball game.

The railroad to the quarries, completed in early 1914, consisted of two flatcars that ran by counterbalance. By the summer of 1914, there were 25 houses in Carrara and numerous businesses. A park was built and featured Carrara's most prominent landmark, a large fountain with multicolored lights that led to Carrara's unofficial slogan, "Meet me at the fountain."

Carrara's peak years were 1915 and 1916. There were then more than 40 buildings at the town site and another camp at the quarry. The population was close to 150. Marble from Carrara won a gold medal at the Panama-California Exposition, but the town's prominence as a marble producer was short-lived. The marble tended to be fractured and not pure, and Vermont began producing large amounts of higher-quality marble.

After World War I, the Las Vegas and Tonopah Railroad shut down, cutting off Carrara. Carrara was now one of the many Nye County ghosts. Today nothing substantial remains at Carrara. The road to the quarries is still passable. The buildings just to the north were never part of Carrara but are the remains of a concrete company, which constructed all the buildings and then abandoned the site in 1936 before production even began.

Very specialized equipment was needed to cut the huge marble blocks that came out of the Carrara quarry. These Chandler cutting machines were top of the line at the time. The quarry was established by P. V. Perkins, who organized the American Carrara Marble Company. The marble mined was prized for its rare blue-white color and won many awards. (CNHS.)

A close-up of the marble wall in the quarry was taken during operations. To move the huge blocks once they were cut, a 65-foot-tall derrick with a 60-foot boom was installed. Part of this is visible on the right side of the photograph. Because the quarry was 3 miles from the railroad, a special railroad spur had to be built. (CNHS.)

A separate camp was built up at the quarry to house the cutters. The workers in this photograph have begun the arduous task of building the double-wide railroad bed for the counterbalance system to move the marble blocks to the railroad siding at the town of Carrara. Construction on the line began in 1913 and was completed the following year. (CNHS.)

This 1913 overview of the marble quarry was taken not long after operations began. Until the railroad spur was completed, the cut blocks had to be put on special wagons and be very carefully guided down the steep grade to the valley floor. There were a number of wagon accidents when the weight of the blocks proved too much for the brakes. (CNHS.)

The quarry camp in 1913 was comprised mainly of rough cabins and not much else. Workers did not mind living in the camp, though, because it was much cooler there than down below in the valley, where the town of Carrara constantly baked under the desert sun. (CNHS.)

Workers are in the process of cutting out the next block of marble during 1913. It was a very involved process. Because the marble from Carrara tended to be fractured, special care had to be taken to ensure that the block would not be damaged. Note the barrels of water. These had to be hauled up to the quarry and were necessary to keep the drills and saws from getting too hot. (CNHS.)

With the completion of the Lidgerwood cable system that used counterbalanced flatcars to haul the marble to Carrara, the camp at the quarry added more buildings, and a small store and saloon opened. Those living in the camp were not really isolated. It was a common sight to see people hitching rides on the flatcars, traveling between Carrara and the camp. (CNHS.)

CARRARA, NEVADA: "TEN BILLION FEET OF MARBLE"
(ONE OF THE WONDERS OF AMERICA)

By 1916, Carrara had become an established town of 150. The town had its own newspaper. During 1913 and 1914, a number of buildings were moved from Beatty and Rhyolite to Carrara. It was much cheaper to purchase a building and move it than to pay for materials to be hauled to the town. (CNHS.)

A 1916 view of the quarry shows the details of its operation. A special tramway was built that would lower the block for loading at the railroad at its end. The ramp at the end was the same height as the flatcars and would roll right onto the cars. It was a difficult process, and more than one block went flying down when the cable broke. (CNHS.)

Carrara peaked in 1915 and 1916. The marble company's payroll was more than $6,000 a month. However, a combination of a higher level of fractured marble and Vermont beginning to produce large quantities of high-quality marble spelled doom for the town. In late 1916, the Nevada-California Power Company curtailed service to the town and quarry because it was not profitable. (CNHS.)

Despite the fact that operations had ceased when the power was cut off, some people did stay in the town for a while, hoping for a resumption of mining. In 1917, the townspeople organized a Halloween celebration. Here Gladys Garrett (left) and friends show off for the camera. However, once the Las Vegas and Tonopah stopped running in 1918, Carrara quickly was completely abandoned. (CNHS.)

When Carrara was at its most prominent, it was a bustling town. In 1915, the owners of the American Carrara Marble Company gathered for this photograph next to the town's hotel. The town had a school, a 1,000-pound-a-day ice plant, dance hall, general store, restaurants, and bars. However, today only ruins and rubble are left at the town site. (CNHS.)

Nine

AURORA

The first discoveries at Aurora were made in 1860, making it one of the earlier mining camps in southern Nevada. Within months, a bustling town had developed, and by 1861, the first of many mills had already been completed. The town was involved in controversy for a couple of years because of its proximity to the Nevada/California border. California designated Aurora as the county seat of Mono County while Nevada had the town as the county seat of Esmeralda County. For two years, until the state border was resurveyed, the town had two separate county courthouses. Finally, Aurora was permanently placed in Nevada. Bodie then became the county seat for Mono County. During this time, Aurora's population rose to more than 2,000.

Aurora's most recognized citizen arrived in 1862. Then still known as Samuel Clemens, the future Mark Twain tried mining and wrote articles for the *Territorial Enterprise*, a newspaper in Virginia City. His entertaining stories were so well received that Clemens was later hired to work at the paper in Virginia City, left Aurora, and soon came up with the name Mark Twain. The rest, as they say, is history.

At Aurora's peak in the 1860s, population rose as high as 10,000 and more than 15 mills were in operation, working the large amounts of ore being produced. The boom had started to fizzle by 1864 as stock scandals and inflated mine values started to impact the town. By the late 1860s, the ore had run out and most of the residents had moved on. During this boom period, the mines produced more than $30 million. There was a revival during the 1870s until 1882 and another short one in 1906 that produced about $2 million.

Aurora has been completely abandoned since the 1910s. For many years, the empty buildings stood in the town, but after World War II, all of the brick buildings were dismantled to salvage the bricks. Aurora is still a fascinating place to visit. A number of partially standing buildings remain, along with a very interesting cemetery, as well as the huge foundations of the Aurora Consolidated Mining Company.

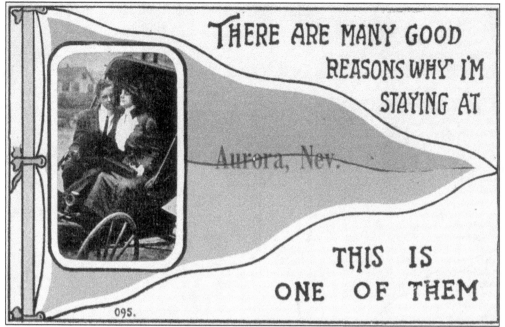

Initial silver discoveries were made in 1860 and a boom developed. By 1861, almost 2,000 people had come. The town was heavily promoted, and this postcard was used to show the human side of Aurora. Hand-drawn postcards like this were used by many towns during the 1860s and 1870s. (SS.)

This is the only known view of Mark Twain's cabin in Aurora. Twain's first adventure to the West was here, where for six months he made fruitless attempts at mining but ended up turning to telling stories to locals to entertain them. When the editor of the *Territorial Enterprise* in Virginia City saw some of his writings, he hired Twain to write for his newspaper. (SS.)

MARK TWAIN 1865 AURORA, NEV.

A group of Aurora's dignitaries poses on the courthouse steps. Mark Twain stands second from the left. After an aborted attempt to make his fortune in the mining field, Twain began writing articles about Aurora under the pen name "Josh" that were submitted to the *Territorial Enterprise* in Virginia City. (CNHS.)

Unfortunately, hardly any photographs exist of Aurora during the 1860s. After 1882, the town was pretty much emptied. By the time this photograph of the Masonic Lodge was taken in 1895, only about 50 people were still living in town. The post office remained open until 1897. The once abundant freight teams hardly ran, mainly bringing in mining supplies for those trying to scratch a living out of the old mines. (CNHS.)

Aurora experienced a revival at the beginning of the 20th century. This new activity brought about 1,000 people back to the town, and Aurora was a bustling town again. Electric power was brought to the town, as shown here in 1905. Many of the businesses along Main Street that had been abandoned for years were reopened. (CNHS.)

This overview of Aurora, taken around 1910, shows the decline of the once bustling town. In the background, the Del Monte Mine and Mill, recently refurbished, overlook the town. Many buildings from Aurora's peak years during the 1860s have disappeared, but most on Main Street still survive. The two-story Esmeralda Hotel, built in 1862, is located up the street with the encompassing veranda. (CNHS.)

This close-up of Main Street in 1910, looking west, shows the Esmeralda Hotel on the left. In the background, on the right side of the street, is the old Esmeralda County Courthouse. Aurora lost the county seat to Hawthorne in 1883, and the building was never used again. Even in 1910, the building stands solid, although all the windows are long gone. This was one of the buildings dismantled for bricks after World War II. (CNHS.)

The Aurora Consolidated Mining Company was the primary company spearheading the revival during the 1910s. Here the impressive mill the company built is in full operation. This was located about a mile from the old town of Aurora. A company camp, called Magnum, was built near the mill for the workers. A number of buildings from this camp still survive today. (SS.)

The Aurora Consolidated Mining Company ceased operations in 1918, and virtually everyone left Aurora soon after. By the 1920s, Aurora's once bustling Main Street looked like this. The gaunt courthouse still stands, but every building was now empty. The town began to deteriorate quickly. Most of the wood buildings were torn down or moved to other locations. (CNHS.)

During the 1920s, this overview of the empty town was taken. All the workings and mill at the Del Monte (7) have already been removed. Some of the prominent buildings left are (3) Esmeralda Hotel, (4) courthouse, (5) Mark Twain cabin, (6) Odd Fellows Hall, (8) school, (9) Girard Mansion, and (10) county hospital. (CNHS.)

The camp of Magnum and the Aurora Consolidated mill were all empty by 1920. More than 30 buildings comprised the little town, and more than 200 men were employed by the company. Once it closed, it signaled the end of Aurora for good. By the end, total production from Aurora's mines was more than $35 million. (CNHS.)

During the 1920s, small efforts were made to restart mining operations. Here, during the 1920s, from left to right, Ben Edwards, Jim Cain, George Ashby, Fred Corkill, and Max Junghandle examine the Junietta lower tunnel. There was constant hope that another big strike would be found, but it did not happen. (CNHS.)

Once Aurora was empty, the remaining buildings in town began to suffer. The intense heat of summer and icy cold winters accelerated the deterioration. By the 1930s, roofs of many buildings had already collapsed, leaving the shell of the walls. Some of the homes were abandoned so fast that everything that could not be carried was left behind. (CNHS.)

During the 1930s, the only people in Aurora were visitors. This couple could be considered two of the earliest ghost town enthusiasts. Amazingly, after all the years of abandonment, the Esmeralda Hotel still retains its sign. Main Street had been lined with buildings, but large spaces were appearing as buildings collapsed or were moved away. (CNHS.)

By the 1940s, Main Street is barely recognizable. The Esmeralda Hotel, to the left, dominates what remains. Soon after this photograph was taken, the operation to salvage bricks began. Once that was completed, virtually nothing was left of the buildings here. The destruction of Aurora was complete. (Southerland Studios.)

At its peak, Aurora had more than 15 mills operating. By the 1950s, this one, located in a canyon to the south, was about the only survivor. It has been refitted and modernized to some extent to be used by prospectors in the area still trying to find another rich silver lode. The ruins of the mills are scattered all around Aurora. (CNHS.)

The present-day ruins of the Aurora Consolidated mill are impressive. The foundations are some of the most extensive of any ghost town. The mill was dismantled, and all of the metal equipment sold for scrap. The remnants of the Magnum are located across the wash from the mill. (SRH.)

Aurora features one of the best ghost town cemeteries in Nevada. It has several different sections mixed within an extensive pinion pine stand. The cemetery is located on a hill overlooking the Aurora town site. There are hundreds of marked and unmarked graves, and the residents there are a cross section of Aurora's glory days. (SRH.)

Here is a current view of the mill shown in a previous photograph on page 125. The elements have not been kind to the mill over the last 50 years. Most of the corrugated exterior has been blasted away by high winds, and the wood frame is struggling to continue standing. However, the original equipment is still intact inside, including an old ball mill. (SRH.)

The one concrete wall of the Esmeralda Hotel is the most substantial remnant at the Aurora town site. The rest of the brick structure was removed long ago, but since this wall had no value, it was left behind. Despite the lack of buildings, Aurora is a fascinating place to visit. By following old photographs, it is pretty easy to locate the sites of the town's prominent buildings. (SRH.)

Visit us at
arcadiapublishing.com

Printed in the USA
CPSIA information can be obtained
at www.ICGtesting.com
LVHW051030011023
759789LV00038B/80